78214
M649b

D0570168

BIG RIVER

THE ADVENTURES OF HUCKLEBERRY FINN

Piano-Vocal arrangements by Rick Walters

Art: © Doug Johnson 1985
Cover design: Winner of Society Of Illustrators' Annual Gold Medal Award

Applications for performance of this work, whether legitimate, stock,
amateur, or foreign, should be addressed to:
RODGERS & HAMMERSTEIN LIBRARY
1633 Broadway
New York, NY 10019

San Diego Christian College
Library
Santee, CA

ISBN 978-0-88188-507-1

Copyright © 1986 HAL LEONARD PUBLISHING CORPORATION
International Copyright Secured   ALL RIGHTS RESERVED   Printed in the U.S.A.
For all works contained herein:
Unauthorized copying, arranging, adapting, recording or public performance is an infringement of copyright.
Infringers are liable under the law.

HAL•LEONARD®
CORPORATION
7777 W. BLUEMOUND RD. P.O. BOX 13819
MILWAUKEE, WISCONSIN 53213

Tree International

DO YA WANNA GO TO HEAVEN?

Music and Lyrics by
ROGER MILLER

Copyright © 1985 Tree Publishing Co., Inc. and Roger Miller Music, 8 Music Square West, Nashville, TN 37203
This arrangement Copyright © 1986 by Tree Publishing Co., Inc. and Roger Miller Music
All rights administered by Tree International
International Copyright Secured   Made in U.S.A.   All Rights Reserved

nev - er get to heav - en 'cause you won't know how. *Huck: And Tom Sawyer wasn't*

above puttin' in his two cents worth either, sayin' I should be more like the fellers in

those adventure books he was always a-readin'. Hey, hey,

Tom and Schoolchildren:

ain't the sit - u - a - tion con - cern - ing ed - u - ca - tion ag - gra - vat - in', and how?

Hey, hey, ya wan-na get to heav-en. Well, you bet-ter get your les-sons or you

won't know how.

Huck: It seemed like ev'rybody in the whole blame town

of St. Petersburg was tryin' to tell me who I should be! Look-a here Huck, do ya

wan-na be a fel-ler, like a fel-ler real-ly ought-a be? I'll

THE BOYS

Music and Lyrics by
ROGER MILLER

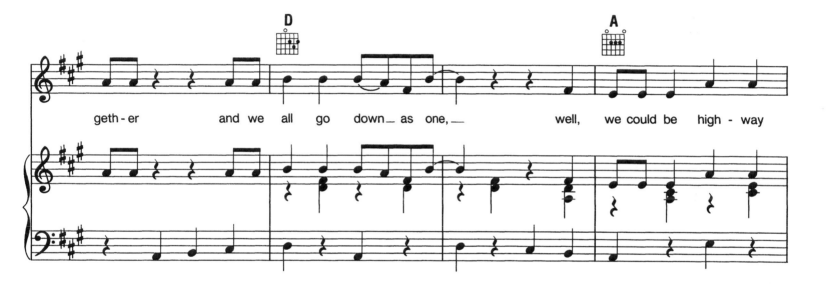

Well, if the bunch of us all___ stick to-geth-er and we all go down___ as one,___ well, we could be high-way rob-bers; we could be kill-ers just out___ to have fun. And if

Copyright © 1985 Tree Publishing Co., Inc. and Roger Miller Music, 8 Music Square West, Nashville, TN 37203
This arrangement Copyright © 1986 by Tree Publishing Co., Inc. and Roger Miller Music
All rights administered by Tree International
International Copyright Secured   Made in U.S.A.   All Rights Reserved

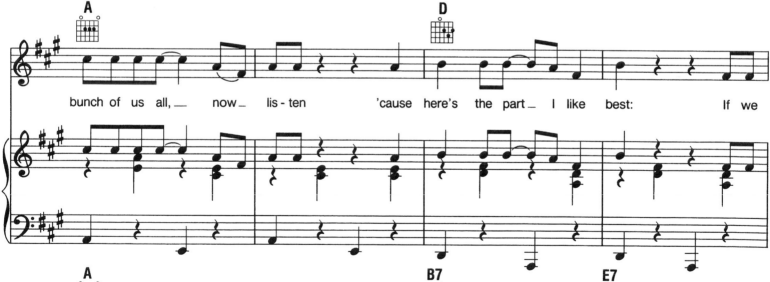

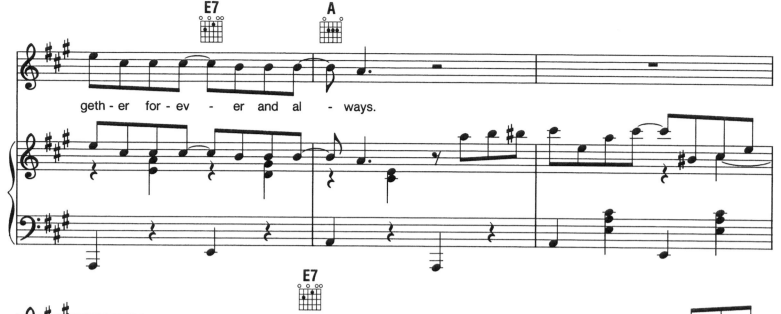

geth - er for - ev - er and al - ways.

Well, if the

bunch of us all___ stick to - geth - er and we all go down__ as one,__

___ well, we could be high - way rob - bers; we could be

WAITIN' FOR THE LIGHT TO SHINE

Music and Lyrics by
ROGER MILLER

Copyright © 1985 Tree Publishing Co., Inc. and Roger Miller Music, 8 Music Square West, Nashville, TN 37203
This arrangement Copyright © 1986 by Tree Publishing Co., Inc. and Roger Miller Music
All rights administered by Tree International
International Copyright Secured   Made in U.S.A.   All Rights Reserved

GUV'MENT

Medium Blues (♪♪ played as ♪³♪)

Music and Lyrics by
ROGER MILLER

Well, you dat gum guv-er-mint, you sor-ry so and so's.— You got your damn hands in ev-'ry pock - et of my clothes. Well, you dat gum,— dat gum, dat gum guv-er-mint. Oh,— don't you know,——— don't you love 'em some-

Copyright © 1985 Tree Publishing Co., Inc. and Roger Miller Music, 8 Music Square West, Nashville, TN 37203
This arrangement Copyright © 1986 by Tree Publishing Co., Inc. and Roger Miller Music
All rights administered by Tree International
International Copyright Secured   Made in U.S.A.   All Rights Reserved

*I oughta tear your no-good, God danged preambulatory bone frame
and nail it to your guvermint walls. . . All of you! You bastards!*

You dat gum guv - er - mint, you

sor - ry rack-a-fra - schitz. You got your-self an itch and you want__ me to scratch__it. Well, you

dat gum, you dat gum,

You dat gum... You

HAND FOR THE HOG

Music and Lyrics by
ROGER MILLER

Copyright © 1985 Tree Publishing Co., Inc. and Roger Miller Music, 8 Music Square West, Nashville, TN 37203
This arrangement Copyright © 1986 by Tree Publishing Co., Inc. and Roger Miller Music
All rights administered by Tree International
International Copyright Secured   Made in U.S.A.   All Rights Reserved

doo doo doo doo doo

In the scheme of things,__ in the way things go you might get bit by the

old Fi - do, but not that gen - tle por - ker, friend.__ How 'bout a hand for the

I, HUCKLEBERRY, ME

Moderately Fast (♩♩ played as ♩³♪)

Music and Lyrics by
ROGER MILLER

Huck: I Huck-le-ber-ry, me some-where sit-tin' un-der-

Instrumental 2nd time

neath some tree some-where, may-be fish-in', may-be

some-where sit-tin' just wish-in' I'm fish-in', oh, I, Huck-le-ber-ry,

Copyright © 1985 Tree Publishing Co., Inc. and Roger Miller Music, 8 Music Square West, Nashville, TN 37203
This arrangement Copyright © 1986 by Tree Publishing Co., Inc. and Roger Miller Music
All rights administered by Tree International
International Copyright Secured   Made in U.S.A.   All Rights Reserved

MUDDY WATER

Music and Lyrics by
ROGER MILLER

Quick

mf

Jim:

C   **Fsus2**

Look out for me, oh, mud - dy wa - ter,

C   **G**   **C/G**

your mys - ter - ties ___ are deep and wide, ___

G7   **C**   **Fsus2**

And I got a need for go - in' some - place,

Copyright © 1985 Tree Publishing Co., Inc. and Roger Miller Music, 8 Music Square West, Nashville, TN 37203
This arrangement Copyright © 1986 by Tree Publishing Co., Inc. and Roger Miller Music
All rights administered by Tree International
International Copyright Secured   Made in U.S.A.   All Rights Reserved

THE CROSSING

Music and Lyrics by
ROGER MILLER

Medium slow, soulfully

C(no 3rd)

Cross-ing to _____ the oth-er side. _____ Mm _____

We are pil - grims

on a jour - ney through the dark -

Copyright © 1985 Tree Publishing Co., Inc. and Roger Miller Music, 8 Music Square West, Nashville, TN 37203
This arrangement Copyright © 1986 by Tree Publishing Co., Inc. and Roger Miller Music
All rights administered by Tree International
International Copyright Secured   Made in U.S.A.   All Rights Reserved

RIVER IN THE RAIN

Music and Lyrics by
ROGER MILLER

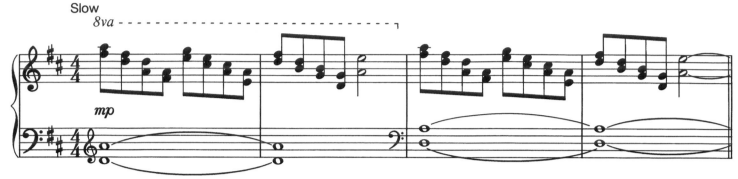

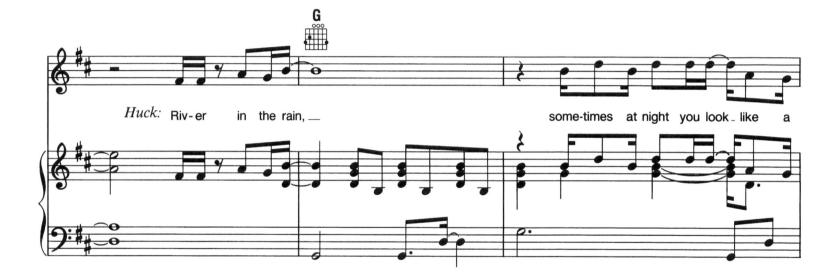

Huck: Riv-er in the rain, ___ some-times at night you look___ like a

long white train ___ wind-in', your way,___ a-way ___ some-where.___

Copyright © 1985 Tree Publishing Co., Inc. and Roger Miller Music, 8 Music Square West, Nashville, TN 37203
This arrangement Copyright © 1986 by Tree Publishing Co., Inc. and Roger Miller Music
All rights administered by Tree International
International Copyright Secured   Made in U.S.A.   All Rights Reserved

WHEN THE SUN GOES DOWN IN THE SOUTH

Music and Lyrics by
ROGER MILLER

Bright Dixieland Swing

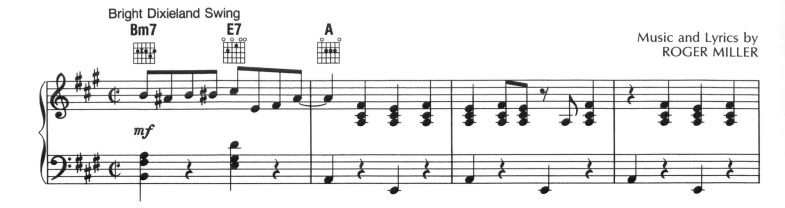

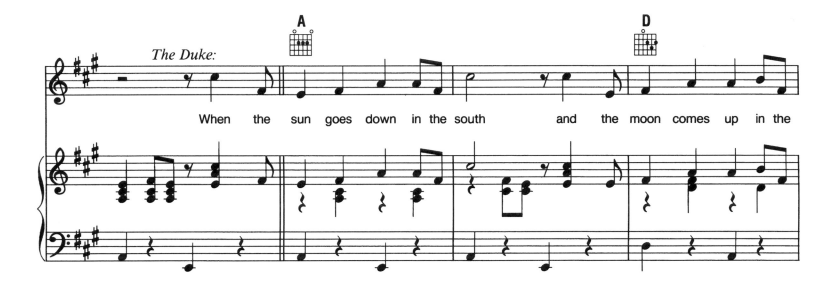

The Duke: When the sun goes down in the south and the moon comes up in the

east, well, step right up and see the won-der of the ag-es. It's a

Copyright © 1985 Tree Publishing Co., Inc. and Roger Miller Music, 8 Music Square West, Nashville, TN 37203
This arrangement Copyright © 1986 by Tree Publishing Co., Inc. and Roger Miller Music
All rights administered by Tree International
International Copyright Secured   Made in U.S.A.   All Rights Reserved

well, you can't im-ag-ine the me-nag-er-ie air___ cre-
at-ed by a cou-ple of guys.___

Duke, King,
Huck:

When the sun goes down in the south and the
hay seeds stand in___ line, we'll step right up___ and see the

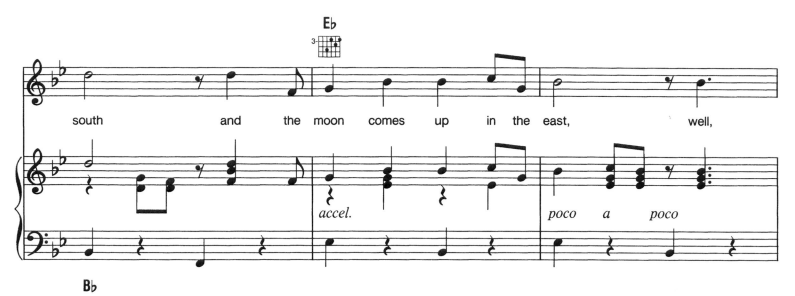

south and the moon comes up in the east, well,

accel. *poco a poco*

step right up____ and see the won - der of the ag - es. It's a

guar - an - teed vis - u - al feast. ___ When the dark - ness falls on the

a tempo

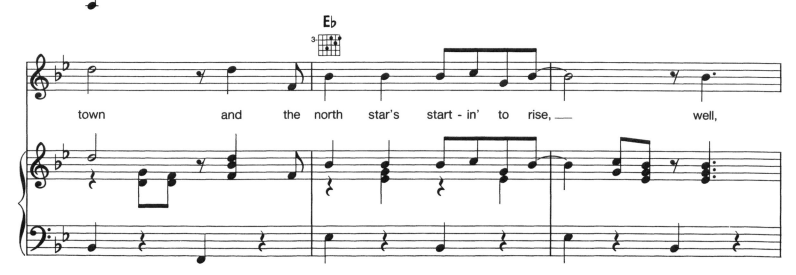

town and the north star's start - in' to rise, ___ well,

THE ROYAL NONESUCH

Music and Lyrics by
ROGER MILLER

Copyright © 1985 Tree Publishing Co., Inc. and Roger Miller Music, 8 Music Square West, Nashville, TN 37203
This arrangement Copyright © 1986 by Tree Publishing Co., Inc. and Roger Miller Music
All rights administered by Tree International
International Copyright Secured   Made in U.S.A.   All Rights Reserved

WORLDS APART

Music and Lyrics by
ROGER MILLER

Copyright © 1985 Tree Publishing Co., Inc. and Roger Miller Music, 8 Music Square West, Nashville, TN 37203
This arrangement Copyright © 1986 by Tree Publishing Co., Inc. and Roger Miller Music
All rights administered by Tree International
International Copyright Secured   Made in U.S.A.   All Rights Reserved

ARKANSAS/HOW BLEST WE ARE

Music and Lyrics by
ROGER MILLER

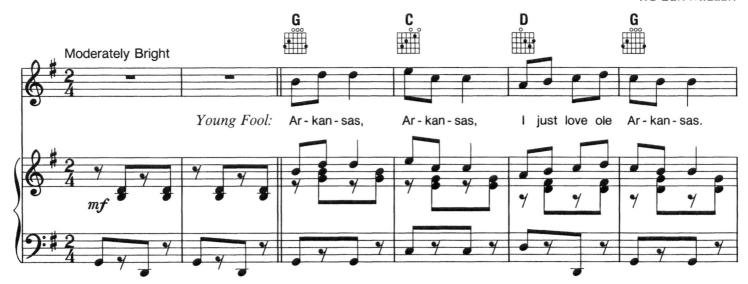

Moderately Bright

Young Fool: Ar - kan - sas, Ar - kan - sas, I just love ole Ar - kan - sas.

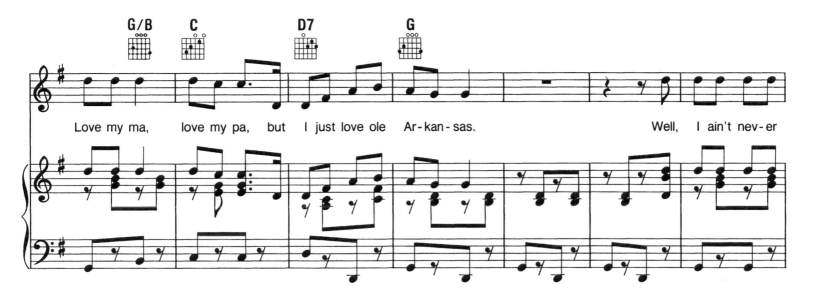

Love my ma, love my pa, but I just love ole Ar - kan - sas. Well, I ain't nev - er

trav-eled much, but some-day when the mon-ey's such I'd like to see the world and all and take a run through

Copyright © 1985 Tree Publishing Co., Inc. and Roger Miller Music, 8 Music Square West, Nashville, TN 37203
This arrangement Copyright © 1986 by Tree Publishing Co., Inc. and Roger Miller Music
All rights administered by Tree International
International Copyright Secured   Made in U.S.A.   All Rights Reserved

Ar - kan - sas.

I'd like to get my pic - ture took and put it in my mem-'ry book and some-day hang it
Grand-pa, he was al - ways good. I'd play hors-ey on his foot and he'd tell me when

on my wall to say that I've seen Ar - kan - sas.
I'd get tall we'd both go see Ar - kan - sas.

Ar - kan - sas, Ar - kan - sas, I just love ole

Ar - kan - sas. Love my ma, love my pa, but I just love ole Ar - kan - sas.

How Blest We Are

(A Hymn)

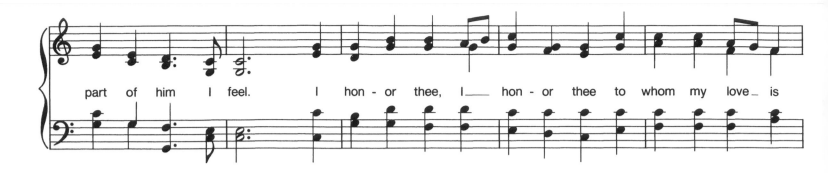

part of him I feel. I hon - or thee, I__ hon - or thee to whom my love__ is

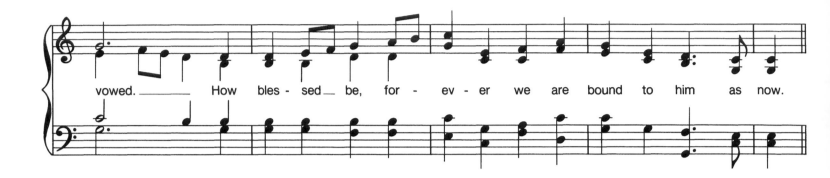

vowed. _____ How bles - sed__ be, for - ev - er we are bound to him as now.

In a black gospel style

Alice's daughter:

How blest we are as child - ren of__ a God so good__ and true, _____ To

un - der - stand his__ mov - ing hand and love for me and you. How blest we are as

child - ren of __ a __ God whose love __ is real, __ e - nough to __ touch, each

one of us __ is part of him I feel. I ho - nor thee, __ I

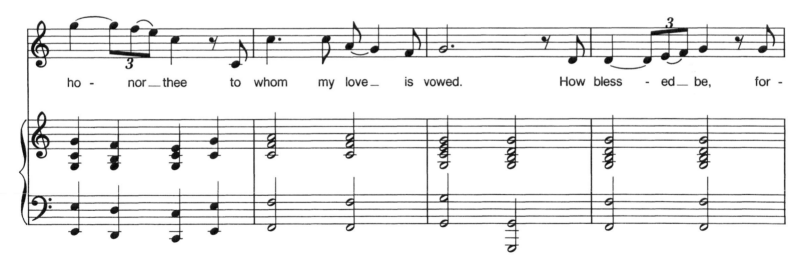

ho - nor __ thee to whom my love __ is vowed. How bless - ed __ be, for -

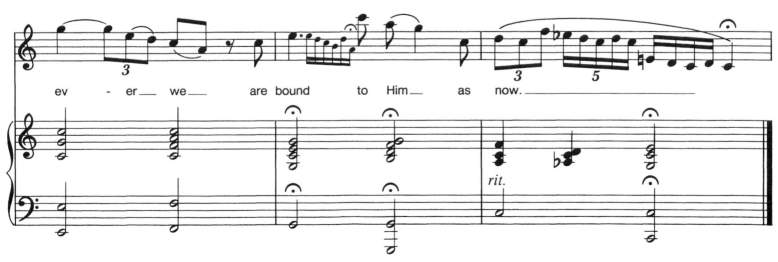

ev - er we __ are bound to Him __ as now. __

rit.

YOU OUGHTA BE HERE WITH ME

Music and Lyrics by
ROGER MILLER

Slow Country Waltz

Mary Jane:

If you think it's lone-some where

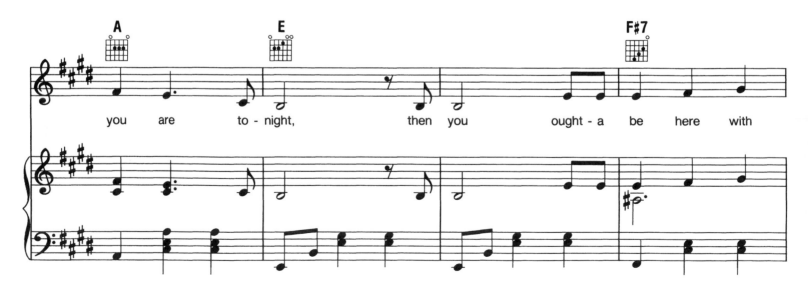

you are to-night, then you ought-a be here with

Copyright © 1985 Tree Publishing Co., Inc. and Roger Miller Music, 8 Music Square West, Nashville, TN 37203
This arrangement Copyright © 1986 by Tree Publishing Co., Inc. and Roger Miller Music
All rights administered by Tree International
International Copyright Secured   Made in U.S.A.   All Rights Reserved

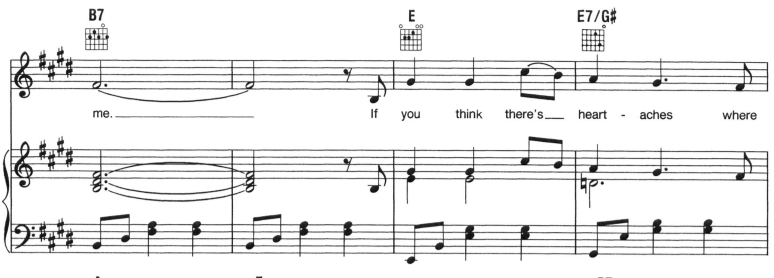

me. _____ If you think there's___ heart - aches where

you are to - night, then you ought - a be here with

me. _____ 'Cause with you I'm _____

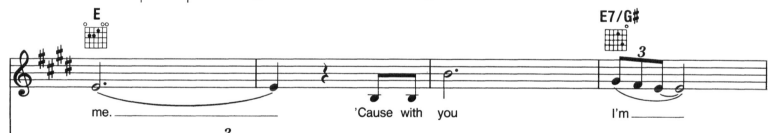

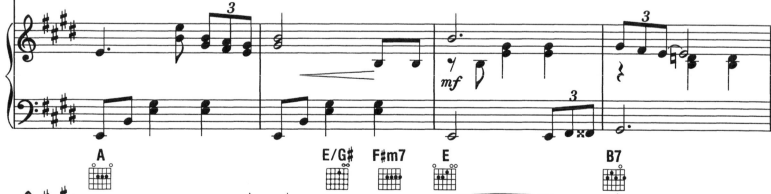

whole, with - out you I'm cold. _____

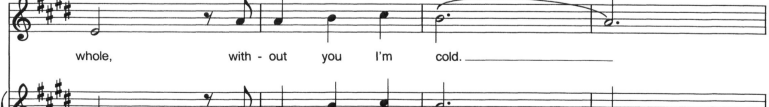

Leavin's Not the Only Way to Go

Music and Lyrics by
ROGER MILLER

Copyright © 1985 Tree Publishing Co., Inc. and Roger Miller Music, 8 Music Square West, Nashville, TN 37203
This arrangement Copyright © 1986 by Tree Publishing Co., Inc. and Roger Miller Music
All rights administered by Tree International
International Copyright Secured   Made in U.S.A.   All Rights Reserved

FREE AT LAST

Music and Lyrics by
ROGER MILLER

Like a slow spiritual

Jim: I wish by gol-ly I could spread my wings and fly and let my ground-ed soul be free for just a lit-tle while, To be like ea-gles when they ride up-on the wind, and taste the

Copyright © 1985 Tree Publishing Co., Inc. and Roger Miller Music, 8 Music Square West, Nashville, TN 37203
This arrangement Copyright © 1986 by Tree Publishing Co., Inc. and Roger Miller Music
All rights administered by Tree International
International Copyright Secured   Made in U.S.A.   All Rights Reserved

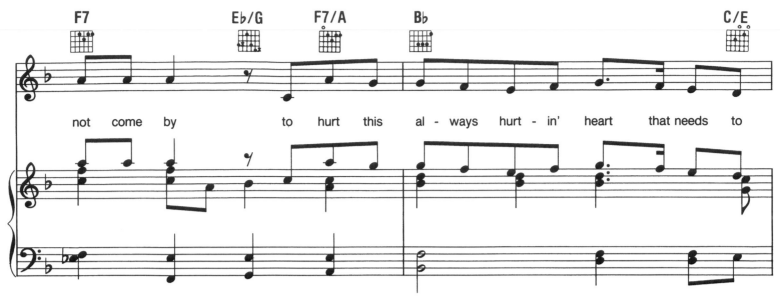

not come by to hurt this al - ways hurt - in' heart that needs to

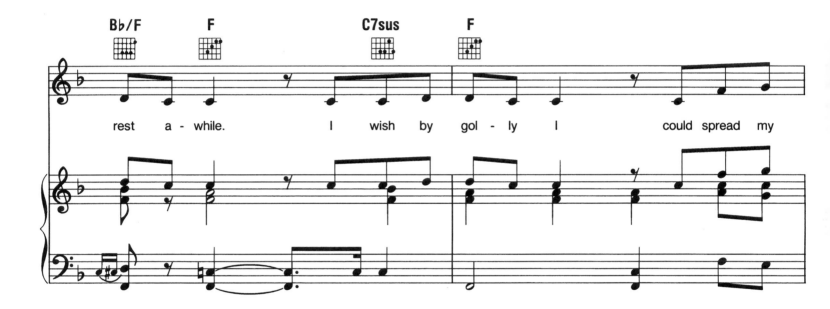

rest a - while. I wish by gol - ly I could spread my

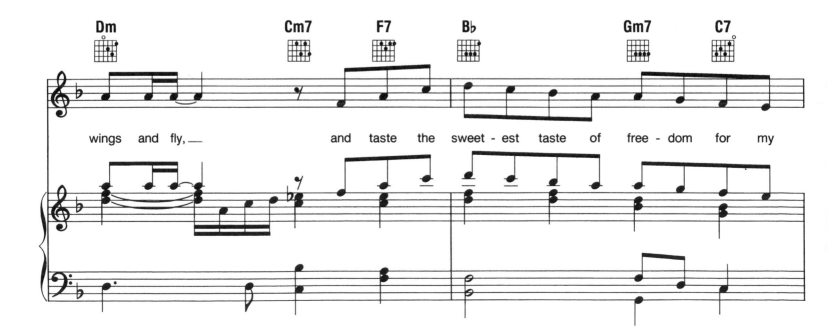

wings and fly, ___ and taste the sweet - est taste of free - dom for my